Dear Parent:

Congratulations! Your child is taking the first steps on an exciting journey. The destination? Independent reading!

STEP INTO READING® will help your child get there. The program offers books at five levels that accompany children from their first attempts at reading to reading success. Each step includes fun stories, fiction and nonfiction, and colorful art. There are also Step into Reading Sticker Books, Step into Reading Math Readers, and Step into Reading Phonics Readers— a complete literacy program with something to interest every child.

Learning to Read, Step by Step!

Ready to Read   Preschool–Kindergarten
• big type and easy words • rhyme and rhythm • picture clues
For children who know the alphabet and are eager to begin reading.

Reading with Help   Preschool–Grade 1
• basic vocabulary • short sentences • simple stories
For children who recognize familiar words and sound out new words with help.

Reading on Your Own   Grades 1–3
• engaging characters • easy-to-follow plots • popular topics
For children who are ready to read on their own.

Reading Paragraphs   Grades 2–3
• challenging vocabulary • short paragraphs • exciting stories
For newly independent readers who read simple sentences with confidence.

Ready for Chapters   Grades 2–4
• chapters • longer paragraphs • full-color art
For children who want to take the plunge into chapter books but still like colorful pictures.

STEP INTO READING® is designed to give every child a successful reading experience. The grade levels are only guides. Children can progress through the steps at their own speed, developing confidence in their reading, no matter what their grade.

Remember, a lifetime love of reading starts with a single step!

*The author and editor would like to thank
Dr. Robert T. Bakker for his assistance
in the preparation of this book.*

Text copyright © 2003 by Universal Studios and Amblin Entertainment, Inc.
Illustrations copyright © 2003 by Michael Skrepnick. JURASSIC PARK is a trademark and
copyright of Universal Studios and Amblin Entertainment, Inc. All rights reserved under
International and Pan-American Copyright Conventions. Published in the United States by
Random House Children's Books, a division of Random House, Inc., New York, and
simultaneously in Canada by Random House of Canada Limited, Toronto.

Photo credits: © Tom Brakefield/CORBIS, p. 12; © Paul A. Souders/CORBIS, p. 13;
© Royalty-Free/CORBIS, p. 25; © CORBIS, p. 28; ALL RIGHTS RESERVED, IMAGE ARCHIVES,
DENVER MUSEUM OF NATURE & SCIENCE, p. 33; Courtesy of Dr. Kenneth Carpenter,
p. 33 (top); © Michael & Patricia Fogden/CORBIS, p. 42; © Mary Ann McDonald/
CORBIS, p. 43.

www.stepintoreading.com
www.jpinstitute.com

Educators and librarians, for a variety of teaching tools, visit us at
www.randomhouse.com/teachers

Library of Congress Cataloging-in-Publication Data
Holtz, Thomas R., 1965–
T. rex : hunter or scavenger? / by Thomas R. Holtz, Jr. ; illustrated by Michael Skrepnick.
    p.   cm. — (Step into reading. A step 5 book)
SUMMARY: Discusses evidence from paleontologists showing that *Tyrannosaurus rex*
both hunted and scavenged for food.
ISBN 0-375-81297-0 (trade) — ISBN 0-375-91297-5 (lib. bdg.)
1. Tyrannosaurus rex—Juvenile literature. [1. Tyrannosaurus rex. 2. Dinosaurs.]
I. Skrepnick, Michael William, ill. II. Title. III. Series: Step into reading. Step 5 book.
QE862.S3 H6535 2003   567.912'9—dc21   2002015735

Printed in the United States of America   10 9 8 7 6 5 4 3 2 1   First Edition

STEP INTO READING, RANDOM HOUSE, and the Random House colophon are registered trademarks
of Random House, Inc.

JURASSIC PARK INSTITUTE is a trademark and copyright of Universal Studios and Amblin
Entertainment, Inc. Licensed by Universal Studios Licensing, LLLP. All rights reserved.

JURASSIC PARK
INSTITUTE

T. REX
Hunter or Scavenger?

by Dr. Thomas R. Holtz, Jr.

illustrated by Michael Skrepnick

Random House 🏠 New York

Chapter 1
The Kingdom of *T. rex*

T. rex as Scavenger

The time is 65 million years ago. The place is the vast forest that will one day be the western part of North America.

Striding briskly through the woods, a *Tyrannosaurus rex*—or *T. rex*, for short—sniffs the hot air in search of its next meal. The *T. rex* is the largest meat-eater alive at this time. Over 40 feet long and 13 feet high at the hips, no other flesh-eating dinosaur around comes close to it in size.

A big meat-eater like that needs an awful lot of food to keep it going. This *T. rex* is hungry. It's been a couple of days since its last big meal.

The *T. rex* stops walking. It smells something on the wind. It is the delicious scent of rotting meat! *Mmmmm.*

Crashing through the bushes, the *T. rex* follows its nose to the source of the smell—the dead body of a duckbill *Anatotitan* (a-NAT-o-TIE-tan). The *T. rex's* mouth waters. Rotten *Anatotitan* is its favorite food!

The kingdom of *T. rex* is full of delicious dinosaurs for the eating. There are other duckbills, like *Edmontosaurus* (ed-MON-toe-SAWR-us). Horned dinosaurs, like *Triceratops* (trie-SAIR-a-tops). Fast-running *Ornithomimus* (or-NITH-o-MIEM-us). There are dome-headed *Pachycephalosaurus* (PAK-ee-SEF-a-lo-SAWR-us) and armored *Ankylosaurus* (ANG-ki-lo-SAWR-us). Long-necked *Alamosaurus* (AL-a-mo-SAWR-us). And a lot more. All of them are food for *Tyrannosaurus rex*.

RRRRRRIPPPP!

T. rex takes a bite out of giant *Alamosaurus*.

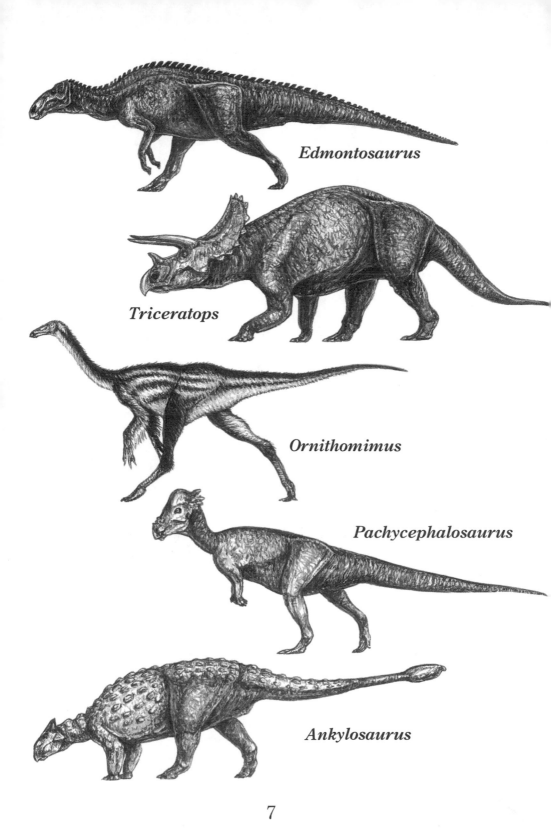

Edmontosaurus

Triceratops

Ornithomimus

Pachycephalosaurus

Ankylosaurus

With each bite, the *T. rex* rips off a giant chunk of *Anatotitan* meat and bone. *T. rex* is a messy eater. Pieces of *Anatotitan* go flying in all directions.

The smell of blood and rotten meat attracts others to the feast. First, flies and other insects show up. Then some meat-eating lizards and a few dromaeosaurs, or "raptor" dinosaurs. Most of these animals wait for the *T. rex* to finish eating. No need to make the big guy mad! But a few dash out of the brush to grab at scraps. None attempts to steal the carcass from the giant tyrannosaur.

The raptors who arrive at the scene are relatives of the vicious *Velociraptor* of Mongolia, the dinosaur made famous in the *Jurassic Park* movies. Raptors are deadly. But these raptors only weigh about thirty pounds each. The *T. rex*'s five-foot-long head alone is much larger than an entire raptor!

And then suddenly, the *T. rex* stops eating. It lifts its bloody snout into the wind. It smells something. Something in the forest that's coming closer. It is the one thing that a *Tyrannosaurus rex* fears—another *Tyrannosaurus rex*! It must eat quickly, or risk losing its meal to the newcomer.

RRRRRRIPPPP!

Did a scene like this ever take place in the kingdom of *T. rex*? Probably. Could the scene have begun a different way? Absolutely. For example . . .

T. rex as Predator

A hungry *T. rex* is striding through the forest. It smells something on the wind. It is the smell of its favorite food—fresh, juicy *Anatotitan*!

The *T. rex* follows its nose to the source of the smell—a herd of *Anatotitan* browsing in a clearing. They are big—three tons or more—but the *T. rex* is bigger. And the "tyrant" dinosaur is downwind. The duckbills don't even know it's there. The

T. rex charges. The *Anatotitans* scatter. One unlucky beast makes a wrong turn, and the *T. rex* catches up with it. It bites the *Anatotitan* on the hip, ripping out a giant chunk of flesh and bone.

The duckbill falls to the ground and struggles to get away.

RRRRRRIPPPP!

The *T. rex* bites down and tears off another huge chunk of meat and bone. As the *Anatotitan* becomes still, the *T. rex* begins to feed.

Mmmmm.

Chapter 2
Hunter vs. Scavenger

We know from the shape of its teeth that *Tyrannosaurus rex* was a meat-eater. But without a time machine, we can't be certain how *T. rex* got the meat it ate.

Many kinds of animals eat meat. From shrews to killer whales, garter snakes to crocodiles, mockingbirds to condors, meat-eaters (called *carnivores*) come in many shapes and sizes.

All carnivores eat other animals, but not all carnivores *kill* the animals they eat. Those that do kill their own food are called *hunters* or *predators*. Those that eat *carrion,* or the bodies of animals that are already dead, are called *scavengers.*

Lions and hawks are examples of hunters. Brown hyenas and vultures are examples of scavengers.

We can watch present-day carnivores and see how they get their food. But what about *extinct,* or no longer living, carnivores

like *T. rex*? *Tyrannosaurus rex* died out 65 million years before human beings were alive, so no person ever saw a *T. rex* feed.

Chapter 3
The Science of Paleontology

Paleontologists are scientists who study *fossils,* the remains of ancient animals and plants preserved in rock. Dinosaurs like *T. rex* are known only from their fossils.

All scientists use observations about the world around us to try and answer questions. Paleontologists, for example, look at the fossil remains of ancient creatures to try and answer questions about how they lived. One question that paleontologists have asked is whether *Tyrannosaurus rex* was a hunter or a scavenger. But because no human being has observed a living *T. rex,* we can't answer that question for certain.

Many people think *T. rex* is one of the most interesting dinosaurs, if not *the* most interesting one. And many have strong feelings about how they think *T. rex* lived.

Paleontologists look at bones, like this *T. rex* skeleton, in order to figure out how extinct animals lived.

Maybe they think that *T. rex* was too scary-looking to be a scavenger. Or maybe they think it was too big and bulky to be a good hunter.

Science, however, doesn't work by feelings. If we want to answer a question scientifically, we have to put aside our feelings. Instead, to do "good science," we have to look at the *evidence,* or clues, that we can find to help answer the question.

That evidence might show that our "favorite" answer is correct. It might show that our favorite answer is wrong. It might even show that there isn't enough evidence to choose between answers.

So let's try to answer the hunter/scavenger question by looking at the evidence found in fossils.

Chapter 4
T. rex the Scavenger?

Some paleontologists think that *T. rex* could not hunt. They think that it was strictly a scavenger. They base this idea on their own observations of its bones. What are their observations?

- Its eyes were small, so it probably couldn't see very well.
- The "smelling" part of its brain was so huge, it probably sniffed for carrion, like a vulture.
- Its arms were too tiny to catch food.
- Its teeth were built for crushing bones and not for slicing meat.
- Its legs were too short for it to have run fast.

In science, a good question is one that can be answered by looking at evidence. Let's see if the evidence really supports this idea.

Chapter 5
Beady Eyes, Dino-brains, and Dinky Arms

Look at the skull of *Tyrannosaurus rex*. At first glance, it looks like the space for the eyeball is really small, especially compared to the rest of the head. Some paleontologists think that this would have made *T. rex*'s eyes too "beady," or small, to see well.

But in dinosaurs—as in most animals— the size of the eyes compared to the head changes as an animal gets bigger. To see what I mean, compare a baby's head to a grown-up's. Or a puppy's head to an adult dog's. Baby (and puppy) eyes are bigger compared to the rest of their heads than are grown-up (and adult dog) eyes.

T. rex eyes faced forward, so that they could focus on things right in front of them.

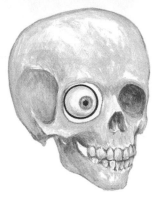

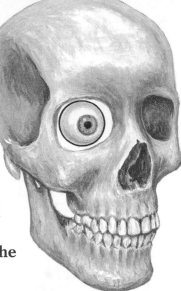

As humans grow from kid-sized (left) to adult-sized (right), the eyeball only grows a little, but the skull grows a lot.

But if we measure the size of the eyes of a grown-up person or adult dog, we find that their eyes are *bigger* than the eyes of the baby or the puppy. The skulls in the older animals have simply grown bigger, causing their eyes to *look* smaller.

The same thing happened with dinosaurs. When we look at fossil skulls of baby and adult duckbill dinosaurs—or at young and adult *T. rex*—we see that the eyes of the young dinosaurs *look* big compared to the size of their smaller skulls. But if you measure the young dinosaur's eyes, they are, in fact, also smaller than the adult eyes.

The same applies for *T. rex*: when it grew from a youngster (bottom) to an adult (top), its eyes only grew a little, but its head grew a lot.

So *T. rex didn't* have "beady" eyes. In fact, the eyeball of an adult *T. rex* was almost as big as a softball. In modern animals, a big eyeball often means good eyesight. This suggests that *T. rex* had very good vision!

Paleontologists have studied the shape of the brain inside the skull of *Tyrannosaurus*. We know that the part of the brain that controlled its sense of smell was enormous! In fact, it was bigger in *T. rex* than in any dinosaur studied so far.

T. rex brain

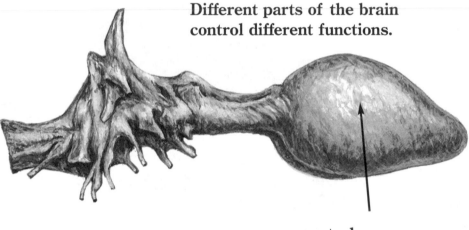

Different parts of the brain control different functions.

controls sense of smell

This part of the brain is also very big in vultures, which are scavengers. So some paleontologists think that *T. rex* acted like a vulture. That is, it sniffed around for carrion to eat.

But just because *T. rex* had a good sense of smell doesn't mean that it couldn't hunt. After all, wolves have an *excellent* sense of smell and they are definitely hunters!

Being able to smell a *living* dinosaur would have been just as helpful to a hunter as being able to smell a *dead* dinosaur would have been to a scavenger. So the size of the part of its brain that "smells" does not help us answer the question one way or the other.

lion   spotted hyena

What about those dinky arms? *T. rex* had *very* short arms for its size. In fact, its hands couldn't reach its own mouth!

Paleontologists who think that *T. rex* was just a scavenger say that its arms were too short to have been useful in hunting.

Paleontologists who think that *T. rex* was a hunter *agree* that its arms were useless in hunting. But just because *T. rex* couldn't use its arms to attack doesn't mean

T. rex

that it wasn't a hunter! After all, modern predators do not all hunt the same way.

Lions, tigers, and other big cats attack by first grabbing their victims, or *prey,* with their arms. They then kill them with their teeth and claws.

But wolves and spotted hyenas hunt using only their jaws. These hunters have powerful skulls and teeth that let them tear at or grab on to prey without using their arms.

Eagles and hawks are hunters whose arms have changed into wings. Snakes are hunters that have no arms or legs at all! So there are *many* hunters alive today that kill other animals without using arms. Just because a *T. rex* didn't have long arms doesn't mean it wasn't a hunter. It just means it didn't use its arms to hunt.

The tooth of a small meat-eating dinosaur. If you cut it front-to-back (look at the black part), you can see that the sides are pretty flat.

Chapter 6
Bone-crushing Teeth and Bite Marks

The teeth of most meat-eating dinosaurs were shaped like steak knives. They were flat on each side and had cutting edges with little bumps, called *serrations,* on the front and back. Like a steak knife, these teeth were built to cut and slice through meat.

The upper jaw teeth of *T. rex*. The black shapes show what these teeth look like when you cut them front-to-back: they are round, not flat-sided.

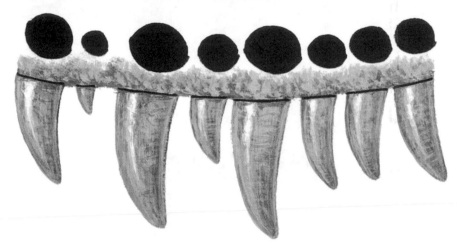

The teeth of *T. rex* and its closest relatives (the other tyrant dinosaurs) were different from knives. Tyrant dinosaur teeth had serrated edges, but they were rounded on each side, like bananas, and not flat. Tyrant teeth were not like steak knives. They would not have been good for slicing through meat at all.

The differences between typical meat-eating dinosaur teeth and tyrant teeth went even further—into the bone, that is. In most carnivorous dinosaurs, the *crown* (the part of the tooth sticking out of the jaw bone) is about the same size as the root (the part holding it in the jaw). But in tyrant dinosaurs, the crown is only half the size of the root. So *T. rex* and its relatives had teeth that were very firmly held in place.

Some paleontologists say that without steak knife–like teeth, *T. rex* couldn't have been a hunter. They think that banana-shaped teeth were good only for crunching the bones of dead dinosaurs. They believe that the meat on these bodies would have been sliced off by the animals who *really* killed them.

T. rex tooth

The crown is only ⅓ of the length; ⅔ of the tooth is root.

Most paleontologists agree that *T. rex* had bone-crushing teeth. In fact, we have found partially eaten *Triceratops* and *Edmontosaurus* bones that clearly show *T. rex* tooth marks. We even have a piece of fossilized *T. rex* poop full of broken bits of dinosaur bone!

Still, we can't tell from these fossils if *T. rex* was scavenging carrion or had killed these animals and then eaten them, bones and all!

There *is* evidence, however, showing that a *T. rex* was able to attack another living dinosaur. This is a fossil of a fully grown *Edmontosaurus* found in Montana. Near the base of its tail there is a big bite mark. The shape of the bite, and the marks of the teeth in the bone, exactly match the jaws of a *T. rex*. But what is special about this bite mark is that the wound on the bone had partially healed.

Only a living animal can heal. So we know that at least once, a *T. rex* bit a living duckbill. Modern hunters often fail to kill their prey. This was probably true of *T. rex,* too.

The duckbill *Edmontosaurus*, and a close-up of where a *T. rex* bit through its bones!

Does having bone-crunching teeth mean that *T. rex* was only a scavenger? Almost certainly not! After all, the most famous bone-crunching carnivore today is the spotted hyena, which many people mistake for a scavenger but which is really a very active predator.

So instead of using its arms to attack—like a lion or tiger—*T. rex* used the power and strength of its jaws and teeth, like a wolf or spotted hyena. Because *T. rex* teeth were thick like bananas and had deep roots, they could hold on to struggling prey without being as easily snapped off as steak-knife teeth. *T. rex* may have had useless arms, but its jaws and teeth were *very* dangerous!

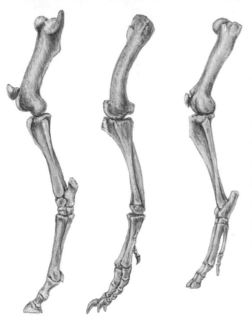

The back legs of a horse (left), a *T. rex* (middle), and a pig (right), drawn as if the thighs are all the same length. Notice how the thighs and shins are about the same length in all three. (Not drawn to scale.)

Chapter 7
Looking at Legs

Some paleontologists think that *T. rex* was not a hunter because its legs were too short for it to run fast. They compare the length of the rex's shin bone to the length of its thigh bone.

Paleontologists then look at *T. rex*. In a full-grown adult, the shin bone is slightly shorter than the thigh bone. This they see as a clue suggesting that *T. rex* could not run. If it could not run, then it could not hunt.

But were *T. rex* legs *really* too short for running?

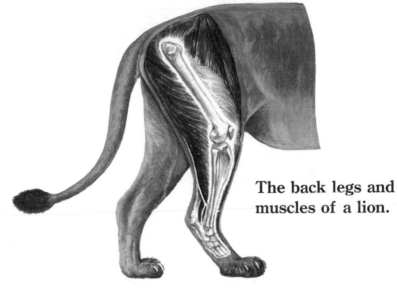

The back legs and muscles of a lion.

In many fast-running animals, like antelopes and ostriches, the shins *are* longer than the thighs. But in a few fast-running animals, like horses and lions, the thighs are a little longer than the shins. And in some *slower* animals, like pigs, the thighs are also a little longer than the shins! The real difference between fast and slow animals is in the feet: fast-running animals almost always have longer feet than slow ones. And *T. rex* has pretty long feet.

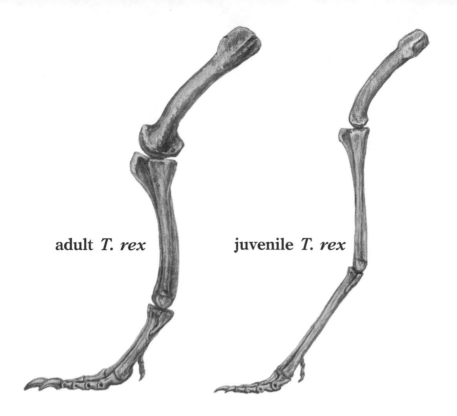

adult *T. rex*　　　juvenile *T. rex*

The legs of a young *T. rex* (right) have shins and feet longer than their thighs. (Not drawn to scale.)

The shape of *T. rex* (and other dinosaur) legs also changed as they got older. In young dinosaurs, the shins were a lot longer than the thighs. The foot bones were also long. But as the animals grew older, their shins and foot bones didn't grow as fast as their thigh bones. Only in the biggest *T. rex* adults is the shin a little shorter than the thigh.

Young tyrant dinosaurs had the same long, skinny legs and feet as ostrich dinosaurs like *Ornithomimus* and *Gallimimus*. Paleontologists agree that the long legs of ostrich dinosaurs indicate that they were faster runners than other dinosaurs of the same size. So young tyrant dinosaurs must have been fast runners, too.

Okay, *T. rex* was probably fast. But was it fast enough to hunt?

The shorter, stockier leg of duckbill *Edmontosaurus* (left) compared to *T. rex* (right). Which do you think was a faster runner?

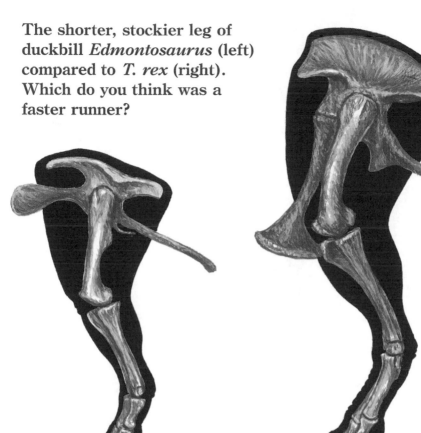

In order to find that out, we have to look at the legs of the animals it would eat. The legs of the duckbills, for example, have shorter shins than thighs. Also, their feet are very short and stumpy. In comparison to tyrant dinosaurs, duckbills have shorter and heavier—and probably slower—legs.

The horned dinosaur *Triceratops*, slower than *T. rex*, but well armed!

The horned dinosaurs who lived in the kingdom of *T. rex* had even shorter shins. They were probably even slower than the duckbills.

So was *T. rex* too slow to hunt? Definitely not! Although we can never know *exactly* how fast a *T. rex* was, its bones were better built for running than those of the plant-eaters in its kingdom. To be a hunter it simply had to be faster than its prey. And that's what the bones show!

Chapter 8
Modern Meat-eaters

We've heard the "scavenger only" argument. We've seen the fossil evidence. How well does the argument hold up? Let's review:

- The eyes of *T. rex* only *look* beady. They were actually quite large.
- The large "smelling" part of *T. rex*'s brain was just as useful for a hunter as for a scavenger.
- The arms of *T. rex* probably *were* useless for hunting, but many living hunters use only their jaws to capture and kill food.
- The teeth of *T. rex* were not good for slicing. But they were *excellent* for biting huge chunks out of struggling live victims.
- The legs of *T. rex* were better built for running than those of any of the plant-eaters in its kingdom.

Based on this evidence, the "scavenger only" argument does not hold up very well at all.

In fact, when we look at modern meat-eaters, we find that very few of them are "only" scavengers or "only" hunters. There are a few that are just one or the other. Vultures are one exception. They eat only carrion. Wild snakes are another. They eat only live food.

Most carnivores in the world today are both scavengers *and* hunters. For example, lions are famous for their hunting skills. But in the wild, lions get one-tenth or more of their food from scavenging carrion.

People tend to think of spotted hyenas as scavengers, but they actually get two-thirds of their food from hunting. In fact, in some parts of Africa, hyenas get nine-tenths of their food by hunting. That's the same as lions!

This shows why feelings are a bad way to do science. We might "feel" that lions are hunters and spotted hyenas are scavengers. But when we actually observe them feeding, it turns out that both are hunters *and* scavengers. If we trusted our feelings without actually observing these animals, we would be mistaken about their lives.

Chapter 9
The Life of *T. rex*

We know that lions and hyenas are both hunters *and* scavengers because we can go to Africa and see them doing both. But without a time machine, we can't watch a living *T. rex* feed.

Scientists make educated guesses about the life of *T. rex* by looking at its bones and comparing it to living meat-eaters. We've seen that the "scavenger only" evidence does not hold up. But that doesn't mean that *T. rex never* scavenged! Of course it did!

We are certain that *T. rex* ate carrion when it found it. After all, carrion is a free meal, and most animals (and people) won't pass up a free meal when they are hungry!

Feeding on carrion is also a lot less dangerous than attacking a living dinosaur. A *T. rex* could get hurt while chasing after a duckbill. Even worse, it could get *killed* fighting a horned *Triceratops* or armored *Ankylosaurus.* But a dead *Triceratops* isn't dangerous. It can't fight back.

And because *T. rex* was bigger than all the other meat-eaters in its kingdom, it could easily chase other meat-eaters away from their own kills.

Did *T. rex* get only one-tenth of its food from carrion? Half of its food? Most of its food? Without being able to watch a living *T. rex,* we can't know for certain.

But *T. rex* definitely could hunt when it wanted to. Remember that *Edmontosaurus* tail with the bite taken out of it? That showed that at least *sometimes* a *T. rex* would attack a live animal.

Paleontologists can even make some reasonable guesses about *how T. rex* would attack.

T. rex would have probably hunted like a giant wolf or giant spotted hyena. It would run up to its prey, grab it with its strong jaws, and rip out big hunks of meat. It certainly wouldn't use its little arms.

Remember the two stories at the beginning of this book? In one, the *T. rex* found some carrion to eat. In the other, it killed an animal for food. Both things happened from time to time in the kingdom of *T. rex*. Just like most carnivores today, *Tyrannosaurus rex* was probably a hunter *and* a scavenger.

Tyrannosaurus rex and its world are long gone, and we will never see one alive. Paleontologists might disagree about how it lived, but we all agree that by asking questions and examining fossils, we can bring it back to life in our imaginations.